Financial Freedom for the Rest of Us

Building Wealth on a Small Income

(UK Edition)

HASSAN AFIFI

Hassan Afifi

FINANCIAL FREEDOM FOR THE REST OF US –
Building Wealth on a Small Income (UK Edition)

CONTENTS

INTRODUCTION

In life, the pursuit of financial freedom is often met with scepticism and doubt. We are bombarded with get-rich-quick schemes and promises of overnight success, leaving us disillusioned and disheartened. But let me assure you, the journey towards true wealth and financial freedom is neither a quick fix nor a magical solution. It is a process that requires time, discipline, and a steadfast commitment to making positive change.

Welcome to a book that seeks to revolutionise your financial future. This is not a guide filled with empty promises or complex strategies that only benefit the privileged few. Instead, it is a practical roadmap designed to empower everyday individuals, those on low to mid incomes, to achieve lasting financial independence. I speak from personal experience and as an investment professional specialising in wealth management, armed with the knowledge that financial freedom is within reach for each and every one of us.

Before we embark on this transformative journey together, it is essential to recognise that creating wealth is not a path paved with instant gratification or effortless gains. It may require some sacrifices, but I assure you, the rewards will far outweigh any temporary discomfort. This subject is of paramount importance, and to fully grasp its significance, we must be willing to invest time and effort. If numbers and calculations aren't your preferred realm, fear not. This book will simplify the complexities, but it does require your focused attention. Have pen, paper, and a calculator at hand, as well as access to the valuable websites we will reference throughout, enabling you to make informed decisions based on your own financial situation.

To ensure a solid foundation, I will first explain the underlying principles that drive the strategies we will employ. By understanding these fundamental elements, you will gain clarity on how to apply them in real-life scenarios. Once the theory is comprehended, we will embark on the practical steps necessary to achieve our financial goals. From accessing crucial information to opening the right accounts for specific objectives, this book will provide you with precise instructions and actionable advice.

It is important to note that this book is specifically tailored for those who have never experienced wealth or feel trapped in a seemingly hopeless financial situation. It is a lifeline of hope, showing you that regardless of your circumstances, there is a path to prosperity.

However, I must emphasise that while the principles and strategies presented in this book are based on sound financial principles, it is not intended as personalised financial advice. Rather, it is an educational resource, equipping you with the tools and knowledge to take control of your financial future.

Are you ready to challenge the status quo, make intentional choices, and embark on a journey that will transform your financial landscape? The rewards may require some sacrifice, but trust me, they will be well worth it. Together, let us rewrite the narrative of your financial story and pave the way towards a future filled with freedom, abundance, and enduring prosperity.

FINANCIAL FREEDOM FOR THE REST OF US –
Building Wealth on a Small Income (UK Edition)

CHAPTER I
UNDERSTANDING FINANCIAL FREEDOM

Financial freedom is a concept that holds immense significance in today's world. It represents the ability to live life on your own terms, free from the constraints of financial stress and limitations. In this chapter, we will delve into the depths of financial freedom, exploring its definition, benefits, and the path towards achieving it.

Section 1.1: Defining Financial Freedom

Financial freedom can be described as a state of financial independence where you have the resources and means to support your desired lifestyle without being reliant on a paycheck or the need to work for a living. However, it is important to dispel common misconceptions about wealth and income that can hinder our understanding of financial freedom.

One common misconception is that wealthy individuals are constantly flaunting their wealth, living extravagant lifestyles, and showcasing their material possessions. In reality, true financial freedom often involves living modestly and making wise financial decisions. Wealthy individuals understand the value of financial security and prioritise long-term financial goals over short-term gratification.

Consider the example of Emma, a successful entrepreneur who has amassed significant wealth through her business ventures. Despite her substantial net worth, Emma leads a relatively modest lifestyle. She lives in a comfortable home, drives a reliable car, and focuses on investing her wealth for future growth. Emma understands that true financial freedom lies in financial security and the ability to sustain her desired lifestyle without excessive reliance on material possessions.

Section 1.2: Common Misconceptions about Wealth and Income

Another misconception is the belief that high income guarantees financial freedom. While a higher income can provide greater opportunities for financial growth, it does not automatically lead to financial freedom if not managed wisely. In fact, individuals with high incomes often fall into the trap of lifestyle inflation, where their expenses increase in proportion to their income, leaving little room for saving and building wealth.

Let's consider the example of Peter, a successful executive earning a six-figure salary. Despite his impressive income, Peter finds himself living paycheck to paycheck, burdened by excessive debt and financial stress. He constantly chases a higher income to sustain his lifestyle, but his financial freedom remains elusive. This example illustrates that income alone does not guarantee financial freedom; it is the management of income and prudent financial decisions that pave the path towards true financial independence.

Section 1.3: The Importance of Mindset and Setting Realistic Goals

Mindset plays a pivotal role in achieving financial freedom. A positive and growth-oriented mindset allows you to overcome challenges, persist in your financial journey, and maintain the discipline necessary for long-term success. It is important to approach your financial journey with the right mindset, recognising that building wealth and achieving financial freedom is a gradual process that requires dedication and perseverance.

Setting realistic goals is also crucial for making progress on your financial path. By setting specific and achievable goals, you provide yourself with a roadmap that guides your financial decisions and actions. These goals should be tailored to your personal circumstances and aspirations. Whether it's saving for a down payment on a house, paying off debt, or building an emergency fund, each goal should be tangible and within reach.

For instance, let's consider the example of Sarah, who dreams of owning her own home. She sets a realistic goal of saving £30,000 for a down payment within the next five years. By breaking down this goal into smaller milestones, such as saving £500 per month, Sarah creates a clear and achievable plan. This approach allows her to stay focused and motivated, steadily progressing towards her ultimate goal of homeownership.

Conclusion:

Understanding financial freedom goes beyond conventional notions of wealth and income. It involves dispelling misconceptions, embracing a mindful approach to wealth management, and setting realistic goals that align with your values and aspirations. By adopting a mindset of financial prudence and harnessing the power of goal-setting, you are primed to embark on a transformative journey towards financial freedom. In the following chapters, we will delve deeper into practical strategies and actionable steps to help you navigate this path and unlock the true potential of your financial future.

CHAPTER II
ASSESSING YOUR CURRENT FINANCIAL SITUATION

To achieve financial freedom, it is essential to start by assessing your current financial situation. This chapter will guide you through a thorough evaluation of your personal finances, including analysing your income, expenses, debt, and how to handle situations where your income doesn't cover your outgoings. Additionally, we will introduce you to tools and strategies that can help you effectively track your expenses.

Section 2.1: Conducting a Thorough Assessment of Personal Finances

Before you can make informed financial decisions and set goals, it is crucial to have a comprehensive understanding of your current financial standing. Begin by gathering all relevant financial documents, such as bank statements, credit card statements, and any other records of income or expenses.

Next, create a balance sheet that provides a snapshot of your assets and liabilities. List your assets, including cash, investments, property, and any other valuable possessions. Then, outline your liabilities, such as outstanding debts, loans, and credit card balances. Calculating your net worth by subtracting your liabilities from your assets will give you a clear picture of your overall financial position.

Example: Sarah, who has been diligently saving and investing, has assets totalling £100,000, which includes £70,000 in various investments and £30,000 in cash savings. She also has a student loan balance of £20,000 and a credit card debt of £5,000. Sarah's net worth would be £75,000 (£100,000 - £25,000). This exercise helps Sarah understand her current financial position and serves as a starting point for setting specific financial goals.

Section 2.2: Analysing Income, Expenses, and Debt

Understanding your income, expenses, and debt is crucial for effective financial planning. Begin by analysing your income sources, including your salary, bonuses, freelance work, rental income, or any other sources of income. Calculate your total monthly income to determine your earning capacity.

Next, evaluate your expenses in detail. Categorise your expenses into fixed and variable categories. Fixed expenses are recurring payments that remain relatively constant, such as rent or mortgage payments, utilities, insurance premiums, and loan repayments. Variable expenses are more flexible and can vary from month to month, such as groceries, entertainment, dining out, and discretionary spending.

Example: Consider an example where John assesses his income and expenses. His monthly salary is £3,000, and his fixed expenses total £1,500, including rent, utilities, and loan payments. His variable expenses, such as groceries, transportation, and entertainment, amount to an average of £800 per month. By subtracting his total expenses from his income, John can determine his monthly discretionary income, which is £700 in this case. This exercise allows John to identify areas where he can potentially reduce expenses and allocate more funds towards savings and investments.

Section 2.3: Handling Shortfalls When Income Doesn't Cover Outgoings

In some situations, your income may not be sufficient to cover your outgoings, resulting in a shortfall. If you find yourself facing this challenge, it's essential to take proactive steps to address the situation. Here are a few strategies to consider:

1. **Increase Income:** Explore opportunities to increase your income, such as taking on a side

job, freelancing, or seeking a raise or promotion at your current job. Every additional pound earned can make a significant difference in bridging the income-outgoings gap.

2. **Reduce Expenses:** Identify areas where you can cut back on expenses. Evaluate your variable expenses and determine where you can make adjustments. Consider reducing discretionary spending, finding more cost-effective alternatives, or negotiating better deals on services such as utilities or insurance.

3. **Prioritise Debt Repayment:** If debt is a significant contributor to the shortfall, prioritise paying off high-interest debts first. Consider implementing a debt repayment strategy, such as the snowball or avalanche method, to accelerate your progress and free up more funds for other financial goals. We discuss debt repayment in more detail later.

4. **Seek Financial Assistance or Guidance:** If you find yourself struggling to make ends meet, don't hesitate to seek assistance. Reach out to organisations that offer financial counselling or consider consulting with a financial advisor who can provide personalised guidance based on your specific circumstances.

Example: Let's say Lisa is experiencing a monthly shortfall of £200 between her income and expenses. She decides to take on a part-time job that generates an additional £300 per month. By implementing a budgeting plan that reduces her variable expenses by £100 and prioritising debt repayment, Lisa successfully eliminates her monthly shortfall. This example demonstrates how taking proactive steps and making necessary adjustments can help overcome financial shortfalls.

Section 2.4: Evaluating the Potential of Starting a Business

When considering financial freedom, starting a business may cross your mind as a viable option. While entrepreneurship can be a rewarding path, it's important to approach it with caution and realistic expectations. Here are some key factors to consider:

1. **Financial Risk:** Starting a business involves financial risks, including initial investments, ongoing expenses, and the potential for losses. Assess your financial situation and determine if you have the necessary capital to support a new business venture.

2. **Time Commitment:** Running a business requires a significant time commitment, often exceeding the hours of a regular job. Evaluate your current work-life balance and personal obligations to ensure you have the capacity to dedicate the time and effort required for entrepreneurial endeavours.

3. **Market Research:** Conduct thorough market research to understand the viability of your business idea. Evaluate the competition, demand, and potential profitability. This step helps you determine if your business idea aligns with market needs and has the potential for sustainable growth.

4. **Business Skills:** Assess your skills and expertise in running a business. Consider your knowledge in areas such as marketing, finance, operations, and management. If there are gaps in your skill set, explore opportunities to acquire the necessary knowledge through training or seek partnerships with individuals who complement your skills.

5. **Starting a Business on the Side:** Starting a business can be financially risky, especially if you rely solely on it for income. It may be more prudent to pursue entrepreneurship on the side while maintaining your current employment. This approach allows you to test the viability of your business idea, generate additional income, and mitigate the financial risks associated with full-time entrepreneurship. For further guidance on transitioning from employment to entrepreneurship, refer to my other book, "Employed to Entrepreneur – Navigating the Transition With Financial Security & Business Success."

Example: John is passionate about baking and dreams of opening his own bakery. However, after conducting thorough research and evaluating his financial situation, he realises that the financial risk of immediately starting a full-scale bakery is too high. Instead, he decides to start small by selling his baked goods at local markets and online while maintaining his current job. This approach allows him to validate his business concept, generate income, and gradually transition into full-time entrepreneurship when the time is right.

Remember, entrepreneurship is a personal journey, and it's essential to carefully assess your financial situation, skills, and market conditions before embarking on a business venture. Starting a business on the side can be a strategic approach to minimise risk while pursuing your passion.

Section 2.5: Tools and Strategies for Tracking Expenses

Tracking your expenses is essential for maintaining financial discipline and making informed financial decisions. Here are some tools and strategies to help you track expenses effectively:

1. **Budgeting Apps:** Utilise budgeting apps such as Mint, YNAB (You Need a Budget), or Personal Capital, which allow you to link your bank accounts, track transactions, set budget limits, and receive spending alerts. These apps

provide a convenient way to monitor your expenses on the go.

2. **Expense Tracking Sheets:** Create a simple spreadsheet or use pre-designed templates to record your income and expenses manually. List each expense category and track your spending regularly. This method offers a hands-on approach and allows for greater customisation.

3. **Envelope System:** Implement the envelope system by allocating a predetermined amount of cash to each category (e.g., groceries, dining out) and placing the corresponding cash in separate envelopes. By using cash, you gain a tangible sense of your spending and can easily monitor how much remains in each envelope.

Example: Suppose Michael decides to track his expenses using a budgeting app. After connecting his bank accounts, he sets monthly budget limits for different expense categories. The app sends him regular spending alerts when he approaches or exceeds his budget limits, helping him stay on track and make adjustments as needed. This example illustrates how using technology can simplify expense tracking and provide real-time insights into spending habits.

Conclusion:

Assessing your current financial situation is a vital step towards achieving financial freedom. By conducting a thorough evaluation of your personal finances, analysing your income, expenses, and debt, and learning how to handle shortfalls when your income doesn't cover your outgoings, you gain valuable insights into your financial standing. Additionally, we explored tools and strategies for tracking expenses effectively, enabling you to monitor your spending and make informed financial decisions. Remember, understanding your current financial situation is the foundation for creating a solid financial plan that will guide you towards a more secure and prosperous future.

CHAPTER III
BUDGETING FOR FINANCIAL STABILITY

*B*udgeting is a fundamental tool on the path to financial stability and eventual financial freedom. In this chapter, we will explore the significance of budgeting, its role in achieving financial goals, and provide practical steps for creating an effective budget. Additionally, we will discuss popular budgeting techniques, including the 50/30/20 rule, to help you allocate your income wisely and maximise your financial stability.

Section 3.1: The Significance of Budgeting for Financial Freedom

Budgeting is the cornerstone of financial stability. It allows you to gain control over your income and expenses, enabling you to make intentional financial decisions and prioritise your goals. Here are some key reasons why budgeting is essential:

1. **Expense Management:** Budgeting helps you track and manage your expenses effectively. By having a clear overview of your spending habits, you can identify areas where you can cut back and redirect funds towards savings or debt repayment.

2. **Goal Setting:** A budget serves as a roadmap for achieving your financial goals. By allocating specific amounts towards savings, investments, and debt reduction, you create a structured plan that propels you closer to financial freedom.

3. **Financial Awareness:** Budgeting promotes financial awareness by fostering a deeper understanding of your financial situation. It allows you to identify patterns, track progress, and make adjustments as needed to align your spending with your long-term objectives.

Example: Consider Hannah, who decides to implement a budget to achieve financial stability. By diligently tracking her expenses and managing her budget, she realises that she was spending a significant portion of her income on non-essential items such as eating out and entertainment. Through budgeting, Hannah gains awareness of her spending habits and decides to allocate more funds towards her savings and investments, bringing her closer to her goal of financial freedom.

Section 3.2: Practical Steps for Creating a Budget

Creating a budget may seem daunting, but it is a straightforward process that can yield tremendous benefits. Follow these practical steps to establish an effective budget:

1. **Determine Income:** Start by calculating your total monthly income, including salaries, side hustles, rental income, or any other sources of revenue. Ensure that you consider your after-tax income for an accurate representation.

2. **Track Expenses:** Analyse your expenses by categorising them into essential and non-essential categories. Essential expenses include housing, utilities, transportation, groceries, and debt repayments. Non-essential expenses encompass discretionary spending, such as dining out, entertainment, and shopping.

3. **Set Financial Goals:** Identify your financial goals, such as building an emergency fund, paying off debt, or saving for a specific milestone. Assign specific amounts or percentages of your income towards each goal.

4. **Allocate Funds:** Allocate your income to different expense categories based on their importance and urgency. Ensure that essential expenses are prioritised, and allocate a portion towards savings and investments.

Example: Let's imagine Alex wants to create a budget. After calculating his total monthly income of £2,500, he tracks his expenses and identifies essential expenses totaling £1,200, including rent, utilities, groceries, and debt repayments. Alex sets a financial goal of saving £500 per month for an emergency fund and allocates £400 towards non-essential expenses. By allocating the remaining £400 towards savings and investments, Alex creates a budget that aligns with his financial goals and promotes financial stability.

Section 3.4: Effective Budgeting Techniques: The 50/30/20 Rule

One popular budgeting technique is the 50/30/20 rule, which provides a simple guideline for allocating your income across different expense categories. Here's how the rule works:

1. **50% for Needs:** Allocate 50% of your income towards essential needs such as housing, utilities, transportation, and groceries. These are non-negotiable expenses required for your daily living.

2. **30% for Wants:** Allocate 30% of your income towards discretionary expenses or wants, including dining out, entertainment, travel, and hobbies. These are non-essential expenses that contribute to your quality of life and enjoyment.

3. **20% for Savings and Debt Repayment:** Allocate 20% of your income towards savings, investments, and debt repayment. This

category includes building an emergency fund, contributing to retirement accounts, and reducing outstanding debts.

Example: Sarah adopts the 50/30/20 rule to guide her budgeting efforts. With a monthly income of £3,000, she designates £1,500 (50%) towards her essential needs, £900 (30%) for discretionary expenses, and £600 (20%) for savings and debt repayment. By adhering to this rule, Sarah ensures that she covers her necessary expenses, enjoys a reasonable amount of discretionary spending, and makes progress towards her long-term financial goals.

Conclusion:

Budgeting plays a pivotal role in achieving financial stability and setting the foundation for financial freedom. By understanding the significance of budgeting, following practical steps to create a budget, and implementing effective budgeting techniques such as the 50/30/20 rule, you gain control over your finances and allocate your resources wisely. Remember, budgeting is a dynamic process that requires regular review and adjustments to accommodate changes in income, expenses, and financial goals. Commit to the practice of budgeting, and you will pave the way towards a more secure and prosperous financial future.

CHAPTER IV
SAVINGS & INVESTMENTS

*B*uilding wealth and achieving financial stability require a solid understanding of savings and investments. In this chapter, we will introduce the concepts of savings and investments, emphasising their importance in securing a prosperous financial future. While we will touch upon certain account types and approaches, the focus is to familiarise you with these concepts. Detailed explanations and further discussions will follow in later chapters. Let's explore what savings and investments are and the basic differences between them, ensuring you grasp their significance.

Section 4.1: Understanding Savings and Investments

Savings and investments are two fundamental financial strategies that serve distinct purposes. Let's define these concepts to gain a clear understanding:

1. **Savings:** Savings involve setting aside a portion of your income for future use, typically in a savings account or other low-risk instruments. Savings act as a financial safety net, providing security and liquidity.

2. **Investments:** Investments involve allocating funds with the expectation of generating income or capital appreciation over time. Investments can take various forms such as stocks, bonds, real estate, or mutual funds. They carry a level of risk and offer the potential for higher returns compared to savings.

Section 4.2: Highlighting the Differences Between Savings and Investments

To effectively manage your finances, it's crucial to understand the distinctions between savings and investments. Consider the following differences:

1. **Risk and Return:** Savings are generally low-risk, offering predictable but modest returns such as interest earned on savings accounts. Investments, however, involve varying levels of risk, and their potential returns can be higher but are not guaranteed.

2. **Liquidity:** Savings are highly liquid, allowing you to access your funds quickly without penalties. Investments may have restrictions or

penalties for early withdrawals, making them less liquid in some cases.

3. **Purpose:** Savings are primarily intended for short-term goals, emergencies, or providing a financial cushion. Investments, on the other hand, are geared towards long-term goals such as retirement, education, or wealth accumulation.

4. **Growth Potential:** While savings help preserve the value of your money over time, investments offer the potential for growth and outpacing inflation, thus increasing your wealth.

Section 4.3: The Purpose and Benefits of Savings

Savings serve several crucial purposes and offer a range of benefits for your financial well-being. Let's explore them through detailed examples:

1. **Emergency Fund:** One important purpose of savings is to establish an emergency fund. This fund acts as a safety net to cover unexpected expenses or income disruptions, providing peace of mind.

   Example: Imagine John, who diligently saves a portion of his income. When he faced a sudden job loss, his emergency savings allowed him to cover his essential expenses until he secured a new job.

2. **Short-Term Goals:** Savings also enable you to achieve short-term goals.

   Example: Laura is saving money to take a vacation to Scotland next year. By setting aside a portion of her income specifically for this goal, she ensures that she will have the necessary funds when the time comes.

3. **Flexibility and Liquidity:** Having savings provides financial flexibility and the ability to cover unforeseen expenses or seize opportunities that may arise.

   Example: Consider Sarah, who saved diligently for several years. When an unexpected home repair surfaced, she had the financial freedom to address the issue promptly without resorting to high-interest debt.

4. **Financial Discipline:** Building a habit of regular saving fosters financial discipline and responsible money management. By consistently saving a portion of your income, you develop the discipline to live within your means and resist impulsive spending.

Section 4.4: Introducing the Concept of Investments

While savings offer stability, investments provide an opportunity to grow your wealth and achieve long-term financial goals. Let's explore the concept of investments in detail with examples:

1. **Wealth Accumulation:** Investments allow your money to work for you and potentially generate higher returns than traditional savings.

    Example: Michael decides to invest a portion of his savings in a diverse portfolio of US stocks. Over time, his investments experience growth, enabling him to accumulate more wealth compared to relying solely on savings.

2. **Retirement Planning:** Investments play a crucial role in retirement planning. By investing in retirement accounts such as pensions or individual savings accounts (ISAs), you can harness the power of compounding and potentially achieve a comfortable retirement.

    Example: Elizabeth consistently contributes to her pension throughout her career and benefits from the compounded growth over several decades, securing a financially stable retirement.

3. **Education Funds:** Investments can also be utilised to save for education expenses. By investing in tax-efficient education-focused investment vehicles like Junior ISAs, parents can set aside funds for their children's future

education costs. These investments have the potential to grow, easing the burden of education expenses when the time comes.

Section 4.5: Risks and Rewards Associated with Savings and Investments

Both savings and investments come with a set of risks and rewards. Let's examine these factors through detailed examples to gain a comprehensive understanding:

1. **Savings Risks and Rewards:** While savings are generally considered low-risk, they are not entirely without risks. One risk is inflation risk, where the purchasing power of your savings decreases over time due to rising prices. However, savings offer stability and preservation of capital.

   Example: Kate maintains a savings account with a fixed interest rate. Although her savings may not experience significant growth, she values the stability and the ability to access her funds whenever needed.

2. **Investment Risks and Rewards:** Investments carry various risks, including market volatility, economic downturns, and the potential for loss of principal. However, investments have the potential for higher returns and long-term wealth accumulation.

Example: John decides to invest in a diversified portfolio of UK government bonds and S&P500 index funds. While he understands the associated risks, he expects higher returns over the long run, which can help him achieve his financial goals.

Section 4.6: Balancing Savings and Investments

Finding the right balance between savings and investments is essential for financial success. Let's explore how balancing these two elements can benefit you, supported by detailed examples:

1. **Emergency Fund:** Prioritising the establishment of an emergency fund is crucial. It is recommended to save three to six months' worth of living expenses.

   Example: Sarah sets a goal to save six months' worth of expenses. Once she achieves this goal, she can shift her focus to allocating more funds towards investments while maintaining the emergency fund.

2. **Short-Term and Long-Term Goals:** It's important to allocate savings towards short-term goals to ensure you have the necessary funds when needed. Simultaneously, investments should be directed towards long-term goals that have a longer time horizon.

Example: Peter allocates a portion of his income towards savings for a down payment on a house in the next two years, while he invests another portion for retirement, which is decades away.

3. **Risk Tolerance:** Assessing your risk tolerance is essential when balancing savings and investments. Younger individuals with a longer time horizon may be more inclined to take on higher-risk investments.

   Example: Emma, who is in her early 30s, has a higher risk tolerance and allocates a larger portion of her income towards investments for potential growth, investing in a NASDAQ100 fund.

Section 4.7: Determining the Appropriate Allocation Based on Individual Circumstances

The appropriate allocation between savings and investments depends on individual circumstances, goals, and risk tolerance. Let's consider various scenarios to guide you in determining the right allocation:

1. **Age and Time Horizon:** Younger individuals with a longer time horizon can afford to allocate a larger portion towards investments, benefiting from the power of compounding over time. Conversely, individuals nearing

retirement may focus more on preserving capital by allocating a larger portion towards savings.

Example: Olivia, who is in her 20s, decides to allocate a significant portion of her income towards investments to take advantage of the long-term growth potential.

2. **Income Stability:** Those with stable incomes and lower financial obligations may have more flexibility to allocate a higher percentage towards investments. However, individuals with fluctuating incomes or higher financial responsibilities may prioritise building larger savings to ensure stability.

Example: Ethan, who works as a freelancer, allocates a larger portion towards savings to have a financial buffer during periods of irregular income.

3. **Risk Tolerance:** Assessing your risk tolerance is crucial when determining the allocation. Individuals with a higher risk tolerance may feel comfortable allocating a larger portion towards investments, while those with a lower risk tolerance may opt for a more conservative approach, emphasising savings.

Example: Sophie, who has a lower risk tolerance, allocates a larger portion towards savings and chooses low-risk investment options such as government bonds.

Section 4.8: Understanding Compound Growth

Compound growth is a powerful concept in savings and investments that allows your money to grow exponentially over time. It involves earning interest or returns not only on the initial amount you invest or save but also on the accumulated interest or returns from previous periods. Let's explore compound growth with detailed examples that include numbers to illustrate its impact.

Example 1: Compound Growth in a Savings Account

Suppose you deposit £1,000 into a savings account that offers an annual interest rate of 5%. The interest is compounded annually, meaning it is added to the initial amount and subsequent interest is calculated based on the new total.

After the first year, your savings account would grow by 5% of £1,000, resulting in £1,050. In the second year, the 5% interest would be applied to the new total, so your balance would become £1,050 + 5% of £1,050, which is £1,102.50.

This compounding effect continues over time. After 10 years, your savings would have grown to approximately £1,628.89. Notice that the growth is not linear but accelerates as the interest is earned on an increasing balance.

Example 2: Compound Growth in an Investment Portfolio

Let's consider an investment portfolio that generates an average annual return of 8% over a 20-year period. You start with an initial investment of £10,000 and make no further contributions.

After the first year, your investment would grow by 8% of £10,000, resulting in £10,800. In the second year, the 8% return would be applied to the new total, so your balance would become £10,800 + 8% of £10,800, which is £11,664.

As the compounding effect continues, your investment would grow to approximately £46,610 after 20 years. Notice that the growth is not solely based on the initial £10,000 but also on the accumulated returns from previous years.

Example 3: Compound Growth with Regular Contributions

Compound growth becomes even more powerful when you consistently contribute additional funds over time. Let's consider an investment scenario where you invest £100 per month with an average annual return of 7%. The contributions are made at the beginning of each month, and the returns are compounded annually.

After the first year, your contributions of £100 per month would sum up to £1,200. With an average annual return of 7%, your investment would grow to approximately £1,246. After the second year, your contributions would total £2,400, and the compounding effect would result in a balance of approximately £2,583.

As you continue contributing and benefiting from compound growth, your investment would grow significantly over time. After 20 years, your total contributions would amount to £24,000, but the compounded growth would lead to an investment balance of approximately £52,396.

These examples demonstrate the significant impact of compound growth. The longer you allow your savings or investments to compound, the more substantial the growth becomes. It underscores the importance of starting early and being consistent in your savings or investment contributions to harness the power of compound growth and achieve your financial goals.

Section 4.9: The Role of Financial Advisors and Resources

Seeking guidance from financial advisors and utilising available resources can help make informed savings and investment choices. Consider the following:

1. **Financial Advisors:** Certified financial advisors can provide personalised guidance based on your specific financial situation, goals, and risk tolerance. They can help you create a comprehensive financial plan, determine an appropriate allocation, and offer investment strategies tailored to your needs. In the UK,

financial advisors must be registered with the Financial Conduct Authority (FCA) and meet certain professional standards.

2. **Educational Resources:** Numerous educational resources, such as books, articles, online courses, and financial websites, provide valuable information on savings, investments, and financial planning. In the UK, organisations like the Money Advice Service and the Financial Conduct Authority offer educational materials and tools to help individuals make informed financial decisions.

Conclusion:

Understanding the concepts of savings and investments is vital for building financial stability and securing a prosperous future. By recognising the distinctions between savings and investments, appreciating their purpose and benefits, managing the associated risks and rewards, and striking a balance based on individual circumstances, you can effectively allocate your resources. Additionally, seeking guidance from financial advisors and utilising educational resources empowers you to make informed choices and navigate the complex world of savings and investments. Remember, a well-rounded financial plan combines the stability of savings with the growth potential of investments, providing a solid foundation for your financial journey.

CHAPTER V
BUILDING A SOLID EMERGENCY FUND

*I*n times of financial uncertainty and unexpected expenses, having a solid emergency fund is crucial. In this chapter, we will emphasise the importance of building an emergency fund, discuss how to determine the appropriate size based on individual circumstances, and provide strategies for saving and growing your emergency fund. By prioritising this essential financial resource, you can safeguard yourself against unforeseen events and secure greater peace of mind.

Section 5.1: Understanding the Importance of an Emergency Fund

An emergency fund acts as a financial safety net, providing a buffer to handle unexpected expenses and income disruptions. Let's delve into the significance of having an emergency fund:

1. **Financial Security:** An emergency fund ensures you have funds readily available to cover unforeseen expenses, such as medical emergencies, home repairs, or car breakdowns, without resorting to high-interest debt or depleting your other savings.

   Example: If your car unexpectedly needs major repairs costing £1,500, having an emergency fund allows you to pay for it without worrying about disrupting your budget or taking on debt.

2. **Stress Reduction:** Knowing that you have a dedicated fund for emergencies alleviates the stress and anxiety that can accompany financial setbacks. It offers a sense of security and confidence in facing unexpected challenges.

   Example: Imagine receiving an unexpected redundancy notice at work. With an emergency fund in place, you can face the situation with greater confidence, knowing that you have a financial cushion to cover your essential living expenses while you search for a new job.

3. **Preventing Debt:** With an emergency fund in place, you can avoid relying on credit cards or loans to cover sudden expenses. By using your own savings, you can maintain your financial independence and avoid falling into a debt spiral.

   Example: Let's say you experience a medical emergency that requires you to pay £2,000 in medical bills. Without an emergency fund, you may be forced to charge the expenses to your credit card and accumulate high-interest debt. However, if you have a well-funded emergency fund, you can pay the bills upfront, avoiding debt and its associated financial stress.

Section 5.2: Determining the Appropriate Size of an Emergency Fund

The size of your emergency fund depends on various factors, including your lifestyle, income stability, and financial obligations. Consider the following guidelines when determining the appropriate size:

1. **Basic Living Expenses:** Aim to save three to six months' worth of essential living expenses. This should cover necessities such as rent or mortgage payments, utilities, groceries, and insurance premiums. If you have dependents or work in a high-risk industry, it may be prudent to save closer to the six-month mark.

   Example: Let's say your monthly living expenses, including rent, utilities, groceries, and insurance premiums, total £2,000. To calculate the lower end of the recommended range, multiply £2,000 by three, resulting in a £6,000 emergency fund. This amount can provide a solid foundation to handle unforeseen circumstances, such as temporary unemployment or other unexpected expenses.

2. **Job Stability:** Evaluate the stability of your income source. If you have a steady job with predictable income, saving three to six months' worth of expenses may be sufficient. However, if your income is irregular or you work in a volatile industry, saving towards the higher end of the spectrum is advisable.

Example: If you work as a freelancer or self-employed and experience income fluctuations, aiming for a nine-month emergency fund can provide you with added security during leaner months.

3. **Financial Obligations:** Consider any significant financial obligations, such as outstanding debt, mortgage payments, or dependents. These factors may warrant a larger emergency fund to provide a more comprehensive safety net.

Example: If you have significant mortgage payments or substantial credit card debt, you might want to save beyond the recommended three to six months' worth of expenses to account for potential challenges in meeting these financial obligations.

4. **Risk Tolerance:** Assess your risk tolerance and comfort level. Individuals with a higher risk tolerance may be comfortable with a

smaller emergency fund, relying on other available resources or insurance coverage in case of emergencies. However, a more conservative approach may call for a larger emergency fund to mitigate potential risks.

Section 5.3: Strategies for Saving and Growing an Emergency Fund

Building an emergency fund requires discipline and a systematic approach. Let's explore strategies to save and grow your emergency fund:

1. **Set a Realistic Saving Target:** Determine how much you need to save each month to reach your desired emergency fund size. Break it down into manageable chunks and establish a realistic timeline for achieving your goal.

   Example: Suppose you want to save £6,000 within one year. To achieve this, you'll need to save £500 per month. Breaking it down into manageable chunks and establishing a realistic timeline can help you stay on track and meet your goal.

2. **Create a Separate Account:** Open a separate savings account specifically designated for your emergency fund. This separation helps prevent the funds from being unintentionally used for non-emergency purposes.

Example: You could open an account with your bank or building society and label it as your "Emergency Fund." This separation helps prevent the funds from being unintentionally used for non-emergency purposes and keeps them easily accessible when needed.

3. **Automate Savings:** Set up automatic transfers from your main account to your emergency fund. By automating the process, you ensure consistent contributions without relying on manual efforts or temptations to spend the money elsewhere.

Example: You can set up a monthly standing order of £200 from your current account to your designated emergency fund account. By automating the process, you ensure consistent contributions without relying on manual efforts or temptations to spend the money elsewhere.

4. **Prioritise Saving:** Make saving for your emergency fund a priority. Treat it as a monthly expense or bill that must be paid. Adjust your budget and spending habits accordingly to accommodate regular contributions to your emergency fund.

Example: You could cut back on non-essential expenses, such as dining out or entertainment, and redirect those funds towards your emergency fund.

5. **Cut Expenses and Increase Income:** Review your expenses and identify areas where you can cut back. Look for opportunities to increase your income, such as taking on a side gig or negotiating a raise. Allocate the extra funds directly to your emergency fund.

6. **Maximise Interest Earnings:** Consider placing your emergency fund in a high-yield savings account or other low-risk investments to maximise interest earnings. Ensure the funds remain easily accessible in case of emergencies while still earning a competitive return.

    Example: Look for savings accounts that offer competitive interest rates in the UK market, such as Marcus by Goldman Sachs or Virgin Money. Ensure the funds remain easily accessible in case of emergencies while still earning a competitive return.

7. **Replenish and Reevaluate:** If you need to dip into your emergency fund, make it a priority to replenish the withdrawn amount as soon as possible. Regularly reevaluate your emergency fund size based on changing circumstances and adjust your savings strategy accordingly.

    Example: Suppose you used £1,000 from your emergency fund to cover an unexpected medical expense. Allocate a portion of your monthly savings towards replenishing that

£1,000 until your emergency fund reaches its original balance. Additionally, regularly reevaluate your emergency fund size based on changing circumstances, such as job changes, family dynamics, or increased financial obligations, and adjust your savings strategy accordingly.

Conclusion:

Building a solid emergency fund is a vital step in securing your financial well-being and achieving peace of mind. By understanding its importance, determining the appropriate size, and implementing effective saving and growth strategies, you can confidently face unexpected financial challenges. Remember, the journey towards a solid emergency fund requires discipline, but the benefits far outweigh the effort. Start saving today and build a strong financial foundation for a more secure future.

CHAPTER VI
DEMYSETFYING DIFFERENT PENSION OPTIONS

*P*lanning for your pension is crucial for individuals at all stages of their careers. It not only provides financial security in retirement but also offers an opportunity to build substantial wealth and enjoy a comfortable passive income. In this chapter, we will explore various pension options, with a focus on Self-Invested Personal Pensions (SIPPs). We will explain how SIPPs work, their benefits, and provide examples of opening SIPP accounts from different providers, including minimum requirements.

Section 6.1: Understanding Pension Investments

When it comes to investing for your retirement, it's important to consider the types of investments available. Here are some key points to understand:

1. **Safe Investments vs Risky Investments:** Safe investments, such as government bonds,

offer lower returns but greater stability. On the other hand, risky investments, like stocks and cryptocurrencies, have the potential for higher returns but carry more volatility. Finding the right balance between risk and reward is crucial based on your risk tolerance and investment goals.

2. **Income-Paying Investments vs Accumulating Investments:** Income-paying investments provide regular income in the form of dividends or interest payments. These are ideal for individuals seeking a steady stream of income during retirement. Accumulating investments reinvest earnings back into the investment, allowing for potential capital growth over time.

3. **Funds vs Single Stocks or Cryptocurrencies:** It is generally recommended to invest in funds rather than single stocks or cryptocurrencies for diversification and professional management. Funds pool money from multiple investors and are managed by professional fund managers. Exchange-Traded Funds (ETFs) are a type of fund that is traded on a stock exchange and normally tracks a specific index, such as the S&P500 or NASDAQ100.

4. **High Dividend Yield Funds:** High dividend yield funds focus on investments that pay out higher dividends. These funds typically

distribute around 5-8% of their value in dividends each year. They offer the potential for both capital growth and income growth, making them attractive for individuals aiming to generate a growing income stream during retirement.

Examples:

- Investing £10,000 in a high dividend yield fund with a 6% dividend yield would provide an annual income of £600.

- Investing in an index fund like the S&P500, which historically has delivered average growth of 10-12% per year, can help grow your wealth over the long term.

Section 6.2: Age-Specific Pension Investments and Fund Choices

Age-specific pension investments take into account your age and the remaining time until retirement. Here are important considerations:

1. **Pros and Cons of Age-Specific Investments:** Age-specific investments gradually shift the investment allocation towards lower-risk assets as you approach retirement age. This strategy aims to protect your pension pot from market volatility and ensure a more stable income in retirement.

However, it's important to weigh the pros and cons of age-specific investments versus choosing your own funds. Age-specific investments offer convenience and a hands-off approach, while selecting your own funds provides greater control and flexibility.

2. **Fund Choices for Growing Wealth:** For long-term growth, index funds such as the S&P500 or NASDAQ100 can be excellent choices. These funds have historically delivered average growth of 10-12% and 14-18% per year, respectively. It's important to remember that past performance is not a guarantee of future returns.

Examples: Investing £100 per month in an index fund tracking the S&P500 with an average growth of 12% per year can accumulate to approximately £99,915 over 20 years.

Section 6.3: Employer Pensions and State Pension

Understanding your employer pension scheme and the state pension is crucial for maximising your retirement income. Consider the following:

1. **Importance of Employer Pension Schemes:** It is highly recommended to contribute to your employer pension scheme. Most individuals in the UK are enrolled in the National Employment Savings Trust (NEST) or other similar schemes. Employer

contributions are an excellent opportunity to boost your pension savings and take advantage of tax relief.

2. **Viewing Pension Contributions on Your Payslip:** Check your payslip to see the breakdown of pension contributions. It will show both your contributions and the contributions made by your employer. Understanding these figures helps you track your retirement savings and take full advantage of the benefits provided by your employer.

3. **Tax Relief and Benefits:** The government provides tax relief on pension contributions, boosting your retirement savings. As a basic-rate taxpayer, you can expect tax relief of 20% on your contributions. This means that for every £80 you contribute to your pension, the government adds an additional £20, bringing the total contributions to £100. Tax relief is typically added automatically to your pension account a couple of months after your contribution.

Example: If you contribute £200 per month to your pension as a basic-rate taxpayer, your total contributions will effectively be £250 with the added tax relief.

4. **State Pension and its Benefits:** The state pension is a regular payment provided by the government during retirement. Visit the official government website to register for an

account and access detailed information about the state pension. It's important to be aware of your state pension entitlement and consider options for maximising your retirement income.

Example: As of 2023, the full new state pension is £203.85 per week. However, individual entitlements may vary based on your National Insurance contributions.

Section 6.4: Understanding Self-Invested Personal Pensions (SIPPs)

Self-Invested Personal Pensions (SIPPs) provide individuals with greater control and flexibility over their pension investments. Here's what you need to know:

1. **What is a SIPP?** A SIPP is a type of personal pension that allows you to choose from a wide range of investment options, including stocks, bonds, ETFs, and more. It offers the opportunity to create a diversified portfolio tailored to your investment preferences.

2. **Investing in a SIPP:** To invest in a SIPP, you need to open an account with a SIPP provider. Some popular SIPP providers in the UK include Hargreaves Lansdown, AJ Bell Youinvest, and Interactive Investor. Each provider has its fee structure, which may include annual administration fees and

transaction fees. It's crucial to compare the fees charged by different providers to ensure they align with your investment strategy.

3. **Opening a SIPP Account:** Opening a SIPP account typically requires meeting minimum requirements set by the provider. This includes minimum initial investment amounts and minimum regular contributions. Review these requirements before selecting a SIPP provider.

Examples:

- Hargreaves Lansdown requires a minimum initial investment of £100 or a minimum monthly contribution of £25.

- AJ Bell Youinvest has a minimum initial investment requirement of £500 or a minimum monthly contribution of £25.

Section 6.5: Exploring SIPP Providers

When choosing a SIPP provider, it's important to consider factors such as minimum investments, minimum contributions, fees charged, and available investment options. Here's a closer look at some popular SIPP providers in the UK:

1. **Hargreaves Lansdown:**

   - Minimum initial investment: £100

   - Minimum monthly contribution: £25

- Fees: Hargreaves Lansdown charges an annual fee of 0.45% on the value of your SIPP, up to £2,000 per year. Additionally, they have trading fees that vary based on the type of investment. For example, buying or selling shares incurs a fee of £11.95 per trade and free for trading funds.

- Investment options: Hargreaves Lansdown offers a wide range of investment options, including stocks, bonds, funds, ETFs, and more.

2. AJ Bell Youinvest:

- Minimum initial investment: £500

- Minimum monthly contribution: £25

- Fees: AJ Bell Youinvest has an annual custody fee of 0.25% on investments up to £250,000. They also charge trading fees, such as £9.95 per trade for shares and £1.50 per trade for funds.

- Investment options: AJ Bell Youinvest provides access to a variety of investment options, including shares, funds, investment trusts, ETFs, and more.

3. Interactive Investor:

- Minimum initial investment: £25

- Minimum monthly contribution: No minimum requirement

- Fees: Interactive Investor charges an annual fee of £119.88 for their Investor Plan, which includes one free trade per month. Additional trades incur a fee of £7.99 per trade.

- Investment options: Interactive Investor offers a wide range of investment options, including shares, funds, investment trusts, ETFs, and more.

4. **Vanguard Investor:**

- Minimum initial investment: £500

- Minimum monthly contribution: No minimum requirement

- Fees: Vanguard Investor charges an annual platform fee of 0.15% on investments up to £250,000. They also have trading fees, such as £7.50 per trade for the first 25 trades per year and £3.95 per trade for subsequent trades.

- Investment options: Vanguard Investor primarily focuses on low-cost index funds and ETFs.

It's important to note that the fees, minimum requirements, and investment options may vary over time, so it's recommended to visit the respective SIPP providers' websites for the most up-to-date information.

By thoroughly researching and comparing different SIPP providers, you can find the one that aligns with your investment goals, offers competitive fees, and provides a diverse range of investment options.

Conclusion:

Planning for your pension is a vital step towards securing a comfortable retirement. By understanding the various pension options available, including age-specific investments, employer pensions, state pension, and SIPPs, you can make informed decisions that align with your financial goals. Take advantage of the opportunities provided by employer pensions, explore different SIPP providers, and consider high dividend yield funds to maximise your retirement income. Remember, it's never too early to start planning for your future.

CHAPTER VII
CALCULATING YOUR RETIREMENT GOAL

P lanning for a comfortable retirement requires careful consideration and strategic calculations. In this chapter, we delve into the process of calculating your retirement goal. By understanding the factors that influence your target amount, including expenses and investment returns, you'll gain valuable insights into how to plan and save effectively. Let's explore the essential steps to help you determine the financial milestone you need to achieve for a secure retirement.

Section 7.1: Understanding Your Retirement Goal

To calculate your retirement goal, it's essential to assess your anticipated expenses during retirement. Start by evaluating your current lifestyle and estimating the expenses that will persist after retirement, such as housing, healthcare, leisure activities, and any outstanding debts. Consider inflation rates and potential changes in your spending habits as you age.

Example: Let's assume your estimated retirement expenses amount to £30,000 per year.

Section 7.2: Factoring in Investment Income

Once you have an estimate of your annual retirement expenses, it's crucial to consider the potential income from your investments. Generally, it is recommended to assume an average annual income of around 5-7% on your pension investments. Keep in mind that past performance is not a guarantee of future returns, and market fluctuations can impact your investment growth. You can work out your investment target by dividing your estimated annual retirement expenses by the anticipated average income.

Example: Assuming an average annual income of 6%, if you plan to retire in 30 years, to generate this income, your investments should be approximately £500,000 by the time you retire (£30,000 divided by 6%).

Section 7.3: Utilising Online Retirement Calculators

To simplify the process of calculating your monthly contribution to reach your retirement goal, numerous online calculators are available. These tools take into account your current savings, expected investment returns, desired retirement age, and estimated expenses. By inputting this information, you can determine the monthly contributions required to meet your retirement goal.

Example: Using the "monthly payment calculator" on thecalculatorsite.com, assuming that you are starting your pension investments today with nothing saved, your target is to reach £500,000 in 30 years, and that you will be investing in an index fund tracking the S&P500, which has historically achieved returns of 10% per year, you need to contribute approximately £221.19 per month into your SIPP.

Section 7.4: Understanding the Significance of Tax Relief

One of the key advantages of pension contributions is the tax relief provided by the government. Tax relief essentially reduces the amount of income tax you need to pay, boosting your pension savings. In the UK, tax relief is typically added automatically to your pension contributions. For basic rate taxpayers, the government tops up your contributions by 20%, meaning that for every £80 you contribute, £100 is added to your pension.

Example: If you want to contribute a total of £221.19 per month to your pension, your actual contribution into the pot will be £176.96 per month (£221.19 X 0.80), and the government adds an additional £44.23 (£221.19 X 0.2), bringing your total monthly contribution to £221.19.

By understanding the significance of tax relief, you can make the most of your pension contributions and enhance your retirement savings.

Conclusion:

Calculating your retirement goal is a crucial step towards building a solid financial future. By estimating your retirement expenses and factoring in potential investment returns, you can better understand the financial resources required to sustain your desired lifestyle. Additionally, recognising the significance of tax relief on pension contributions empowers you to optimise your savings. Armed with this knowledge, you can now move forward confidently, armed with a clear understanding of your retirement target and the steps needed to reach it.

CHAPTER VIII
MANAGING DEBT & GETTING OUT OF THE HOLE

*M*anaging debt and finding your way out of financial challenges is a pressing concern for many individuals. The weight of debt can be overwhelming, impacting not only your financial stability but also your peace of mind. In this chapter, we will explore effective strategies for managing and reducing debt, provide tips for negotiating with creditors, and emphasise the importance of making temporary sacrifices for long-term financial stability. By implementing these strategies and taking control of your debt, you can pave the way towards a brighter and debt-free future.

Section 8.1: Strategies for Managing and Reducing Debt

Debt can accumulate quickly and become a burden on your financial well-being. Here are some strategies to effectively manage and reduce debt:

1. **Assess Your Debt:** Start by understanding the full extent of your debt. List all your debts, including credit cards, loans, and overdrafts. Note the outstanding balance, interest rates, and minimum payments for each.

2. **Create a Budget:** Develop a realistic budget to track your income and expenses. Identify areas where you can cut back on discretionary spending and allocate more funds towards debt repayment.

3. **Prioritise High-Interest Debt:** Focus on paying off high-interest debt first, as it accumulates more interest over time. Allocate extra funds towards these debts while making minimum payments on others.

4. **Snowball or Avalanche Method:** Consider using the snowball or avalanche method to accelerate your debt repayment. With the snowball method, start by paying off the smallest debt first and then snowball the payments towards larger debts. The avalanche method involves tackling the debt with the highest interest rate first and then moving on to the next.

5. **Negotiate with Creditors:** Reach out to your creditors and explore options for negotiating lower interest rates or more favourable repayment terms. They may be willing to work with you if they see your commitment to paying off the debt.

6. **Consolidate Debt:** Explore the possibility of consolidating your debts into a single loan or balance transfer credit card with a lower interest rate. This can simplify your payments and potentially save you money on interest charges.

7. **Seek Professional Help:** If your debt situation feels overwhelming, consider seeking guidance from a reputable credit counselling agency or financial advisor. They can provide expert advice tailored to your specific circumstances.

Section 8.2: Tips for Negotiating with Creditors

Negotiating with creditors can be intimidating, but it is a crucial step in managing your debt effectively. Consider the following tips when negotiating with creditors:

1. **Communication is Key:** Reach out to your creditors and explain your financial situation honestly. Be proactive in discussing possible options for repayment.

2. **Offer a Realistic Repayment Plan:** Present a repayment plan that is realistic and demonstrates your commitment to clearing the debt. Show how you will allocate funds towards repayment while meeting your other financial obligations.

3. **Request Lower Interest Rates:** Ask your creditors if they can reduce the interest rates on your debts. A lower interest rate can significantly reduce the total amount you owe over time.

4. **Explore Debt Settlement:** In some cases, creditors may be willing to accept a lump sum payment that is less than the total debt owed. Explore the possibility of a debt settlement arrangement, but be aware of the potential impact on your credit score.

5. **Get Agreements in Writing:** Whenever you reach a resolution or make payment arrangements, ensure that you get the agreements in writing. This will protect you and provide documentation of the agreed-upon terms.

Section 8.3: Making Temporary Sacrifices for Long-Term Financial Stability

Getting out of debt often requires making temporary sacrifices to achieve long-term financial stability. Consider the following:

1. **Cut Back on Discretionary Spending:** Identify areas where you can reduce discretionary spending, such as eating out, entertainment, or non-essential purchases. Redirect those funds towards debt repayment.

2. **Increase Your Income:** Explore opportunities to boost your income, such as taking on a side gig, freelancing, or seeking a raise at work. The additional income can accelerate your debt repayment.

3. **Create a Debt Repayment Plan:** Develop a clear and structured debt repayment plan. Set specific goals and timelines for paying off each debt, and monitor your progress along the way.

4. **Seek Support:** Share your debt repayment journey with family and friends who can offer encouragement and accountability. Consider joining support groups or online communities where you can connect with others facing similar challenges.

Conclusion:

Taking control of your debt is a pivotal step towards achieving financial freedom and peace of mind. By implementing effective strategies, negotiating with creditors, and making temporary sacrifices, you can regain control of your finances and work towards a debt-free future. Remember, it may require patience, discipline, and a willingness to make tough choices, but the rewards of financial stability and freedom are well worth the effort. Start your journey towards debt management today and pave the way for a stronger and more secure financial future.

CHAPTER IX
SAVING FOR A HOME

*O*wning a home is a significant milestone for many individuals, representing stability, security, and a place to call their own. However, saving for a home deposit can be a daunting task. In this chapter, we will delve into the world of affordable home ownership schemes and government assistance programs designed to help aspiring homeowners. We will explore the concept of shared ownership and its benefits, along with practical tips on how to save for a home deposit using suitable accounts like Lifetime ISAs. By understanding the available options and implementing effective savings strategies, you can turn your dream of homeownership into a reality.

Section 9.1: Affordable Home Ownership Schemes

1. **Shared Ownership:** Shared Ownership enables individuals to purchase a portion of a property, typically between 25% and 75%, and pay rent on the remaining share. For example,

you could purchase a 50% share of a property valued at £200,000, with a deposit of £10,000, and pay rent on the remaining 50%.

Example: John purchases a 40% share of a flat valued at £250,000 through a shared ownership scheme. He pays a deposit of £10,000 and pays rent on the remaining 60% of the property.

2. **Right to Buy:** The Right to Buy scheme allows eligible council and housing association tenants to purchase their rented property at a discounted price. This scheme provides an opportunity for tenants to become homeowners and build equity.

    Example: Sarah has been a council tenant for several years and exercises her Right to Buy, purchasing her rented property at a discounted price of £120,000.

Section 9.2: Government Assistance Programmes

1. **First Home Fund:** The First Home Fund is a government programme that offers a shared equity loan towards the purchase of a property. Eligible buyers can receive up to £25,000 or 15% of the property's value, whichever is lower, as a loan from the government.

    Example: Robert is eligible for the First Home Fund and receives a shared equity loan of

£15,000 towards the purchase of his first property, valued at £100,000.

2. **Stamp Duty Relief:** The government provides stamp duty relief for first-time buyers, reducing or eliminating the tax payable on the purchase of a property below a certain threshold. This relief can significantly reduce the upfront costs of buying a home.

   Example: Emma purchases her first property for £250,000, benefiting from stamp duty relief and saving £2,500 in taxes.

Section 9.3: Shared Ownership: A Path to Homeownership

1. **Gradual Ownership Increase:** With shared ownership, you can start by purchasing a share of a property and gradually increase your ownership over time through a process known as "staircasing." This allows you to buy additional shares of the property when you're financially ready.

   Example: Mark purchases a 40% share of a shared ownership property and decides to staircase to increase his ownership to 60% after a few years.

2. **Rent Payments:** In addition to mortgage payments, shared ownership requires paying rent on the remaining share of the property.

This rent is typically set at a below-market rate, making it more affordable for homeowners.

Example: Laura owns a 60% share of a shared ownership property and pays rent on the remaining 40% share. Her monthly rent is £250, significantly lower than the rental market rate for a similar property.

Section 9.4: Saving for a Home Deposit

1. **Lifetime ISA (LISA):** A LISA is a tax-efficient savings account designed for those saving for their first home or retirement. Individuals aged 18 to 39 can open a LISA and contribute up to £4,000 per tax year. The government adds a 25% bonus on contributions, helping to boost your savings.

   Example: Michael opens a Lifetime ISA and contributes £2,000 per year. The government adds a 25% bonus of £500, increasing his savings to £2,500 annually.

2. **Regular Savings Accounts:** Regular savings accounts provide a flexible and accessible way to save for a home deposit. These accounts typically offer competitive interest rates and allow you to make regular contributions.

   Example: Rachel sets up a regular savings account and saves £200 per month for her home deposit. After two years, she accumulates £4,800, which she can use towards her home purchase.

Conclusion:

Saving for a home deposit requires careful planning, utilising government assistance programmes, and exploring affordable home ownership schemes. Shared ownership provides a pathway to homeownership with a lower initial deposit, while government programmes like the First Home Fund and stamp duty relief offer financial support. By leveraging suitable savings accounts like Lifetime ISAs and regular savings accounts, you can steadily build your home deposit. Remember, each step you take towards saving for your home brings you closer to achieving your homeownership dreams.

CHAPTER X
SAVING FOR OTHER GOALS &
PURCHASES

*S*aving for goals and purchases beyond homeownership is an essential part of financial planning. Whether you have short-term goals like a dream holiday or future purchases in mind, having a solid savings strategy can help you achieve them. In this chapter, we will explore effective strategies for saving for these goals, along with suitable savings vehicles such as cash ISAs and stocks and shares ISAs. We will also highlight the flexibility of stocks and shares ISAs for long-term savings and the potential they offer for early retirement. By implementing these strategies, you can ensure that your hard-earned money is working towards fulfilling your aspirations.

Section 10.1: Saving for Short-Term Goals

When it comes to short-term goals, such as a dream holiday or a future purchase, it's important to have a targeted savings approach. Here are some strategies to help you save effectively:

1. **Goal Setting:** Start by clearly defining your short-term goals and the amount of money you need to save. This will give you a specific target to work towards.

    Example: Sarah wants to save £3,000 for a trip to her dream destination, which includes flights, accommodation, and expenses.

2. **Budgeting and Expense Tracking:** Analyse your current income and expenses to identify areas where you can cut back and save more towards your short-term goals. Create a budget and track your expenses diligently to stay on top of your spending habits.

    Example: John examines his monthly expenses and finds that he can reduce his dining out expenses by cooking more meals at home, saving an additional £200 per month.

Section 10.2: Cash ISAs for Short-Term Savings

Cash ISAs offer a tax-efficient way to save money, making them suitable for short-term savings goals. Here's what you need to know about using cash ISAs:

1. **Cash ISA Benefits:** Cash ISAs allow you to save money without paying tax on the interest

earned. They are a safe and reliable option for short-term savings goals where preservation of capital is a priority.

Example: Emma opens a cash ISA and saves £5,000 for a future home renovation project. She earns interest on her savings without having to pay tax on the earnings.

2. **Interest Rates and Access:** Compare different cash ISA providers to find the best interest rates available. Consider whether you need instant access to your savings or are willing to lock them away for a fixed term. Keep in mind that interest rates can vary and impact your overall savings growth.

   Example: David chooses a cash ISA with a competitive interest rate of 2.5% that allows him to withdraw his savings without penalty if needed.

Section 10.3: Stocks and Shares ISAs for Long-Term Savings

Stocks and shares ISAs offer the potential for higher returns over the long term, making them suitable for saving towards goals that are further in the future. Here's what you should know about utilising stocks and shares ISAs:

1. **Growth Potential:** Stocks and shares ISAs provide an opportunity for capital growth and

higher returns compared to cash ISAs. They are ideal for long-term savings goals such as early retirement or funding major life events. You should approach investing in this account in a similar manner to your investments in a SIPP.

Example: Laura opens a stocks and shares ISA and invests in a diversified portfolio of low-cost index funds. She aims to grow her savings for early retirement in 20 years.

2. **Risk and Volatility:** Understand that investing in stocks and shares ISAs carries risks, including the potential for loss of capital. It is important to have a long-term investment horizon and be prepared for market fluctuations. Diversification and regular reviews of your investment portfolio are key.

    Example: Mark allocates a portion of his stocks and shares ISA to a mix of low-risk bonds and high-growth funds, ensuring a balanced approach that matches his risk tolerance.

Conclusion:

Saving for short-term goals and future purchases requires a tailored approach that aligns with your financial aspirations. By setting clear goals, budgeting effectively, and utilising suitable savings vehicles like cash ISAs and stocks and shares ISAs, you can make steady progress towards achieving these goals. Cash ISAs offer tax-efficient savings for short-term goals, while stocks and shares ISAs provide growth potential for long-term savings and even early retirement. Remember, with proper planning and discipline, you can turn your dreams and aspirations into tangible realities.

CHAPTER XI
MAXIMISING WINDFALL OPPORTUNITIES

*U*nexpected financial windfalls, such as inheritances, bonuses, or unexpected gains, can provide a unique opportunity to accelerate your financial journey. In this chapter, we will explore strategies for maximising these windfall opportunities, allowing you to make the most of sudden influxes of money. By making wise financial decisions, you can expedite your wealth-building efforts, achieve your financial goals, and strike a balance between practical choices and enjoying the present.

Section 11.1: Making the Most of Inheritances

Inheritances can provide a significant financial boost. Here are some key considerations for maximising the value of an inheritance:

1. **Evaluate Your Financial Situation:** Assess your current financial goals, debts, and savings

before deciding how to allocate the inheritance. Prioritise paying off high-interest debts and establishing an emergency fund.

Example: John receives an inheritance of £50,000. He pays off his credit card debt, sets aside three months' worth of living expenses in an emergency fund, and allocates the remaining funds towards long-term investments.

2. **Seek Professional Advice:** Consider consulting with a financial advisor or estate planner to make informed decisions about tax implications, investment opportunities, and wealth preservation.

    Example: Sarah engages a financial advisor who helps her understand the tax implications of her inheritance and suggests tax-efficient investment options.

Section 11.2: Leveraging Bonuses for Financial Growth

Bonuses can provide a significant boost to your financial well-being. Here's how you can leverage them effectively:

1. **Set Clear Financial Goals:** Determine your financial priorities and allocate a portion of your bonus towards achieving those goals. This could include paying off debts, saving for a

down payment, or investing for long-term growth.

Example: Emma receives a bonus of £10,000. She decides to allocate 50% towards paying off her student loan and the remaining 50% towards her retirement savings.

2. **Balance Enjoyment and Financial Prudence:** While it's important to celebrate your achievements, consider striking a balance between treating yourself and making responsible financial decisions. Allocate a portion of the bonus towards a small indulgence while ensuring the majority is used wisely.

    Example: David treats himself to a well-deserved vacation with a portion of his bonus, and the rest goes towards building his emergency fund and investing for his child's education.

Section 11.3: Finding Joy in Small Treats Along the Way

Achieving financial goals shouldn't be solely focused on long-term objectives. It's essential to find joy in small treats along the way. Here's how:

1. **Create a Rewards System:** Set milestones along your financial journey and reward yourself when you achieve them. It could be a

small indulgence, an experience, or a special purchase that brings you joy.

Example: Laura treats herself to a spa day or a night out with friends whenever she reaches a savings milestone or achieves a significant financial goal.

2. **Embrace a Balanced Approach:** Recognise that enjoying small treats along the way doesn't mean compromising your long-term financial stability. Budget for occasional indulgences while staying committed to your saving and investing goals.

Example: Mark sets aside a small portion of his monthly budget for dining out or buying a new book, allowing himself to enjoy these treats guilt-free.

Conclusion:

Maximising windfall opportunities is a valuable skill that can accelerate your financial journey. By strategically managing inheritances, leveraging bonuses, and finding joy in small treats along the way, you can make the most of unexpected financial windfalls. Remember to strike a balance between practical financial decisions and enjoying the present, ensuring your financial well-being while embracing life's pleasures.

CHAPTER XII
BUILDING GENERATIONAL WEALTH

*B*uilding generational wealth is a critical aspect of long-term financial planning. By strategically planning for beneficiaries and effectively passing on wealth, you can create a lasting legacy for future generations. In this chapter, we will explore the key considerations and strategies for building generational wealth. We'll delve into setting up accounts for children, such as Junior ISAs and Junior SIPPs, and provide guidance on transitioning these accounts to standard ISAs and SIPPs when they reach adulthood.

Section 12.1: Planning for Beneficiaries and Inheritance

Planning for beneficiaries and inheritance involves thoughtful decision-making to ensure a smooth transfer of wealth. Here's what you need to know:

1. **Estate Planning:** Create a comprehensive estate plan that includes a will, trusts, and power of attorney. This ensures your assets are distributed according to your wishes and minimises potential inheritance tax liabilities.

    Example: Sarah consults an estate planning attorney to draft her will, establish a trust for her children, and appoint a trusted individual as power of attorney.

2. **Beneficiary Designations:** Review and update beneficiary designations on insurance policies, pensions, and investment accounts to ensure they align with your current intentions.

    Example: John ensures that his life insurance policy's beneficiary designation is updated to include his children as primary beneficiaries.

Section 12.2: Junior ISAs and Junior SIPPs

Setting up accounts for children, such as Junior ISAs and Junior SIPPs, can lay the foundation for their financial future. Here's what you need to know:

1. **Junior ISAs:** Explore the benefits of Junior ISAs, which allow tax-efficient saving and investing for children under the age of 18.

    Example: Emma took a proactive step towards securing her child's future by opening a Junior

Stocks and Shares ISA. Every month, she diligently contributed £100, investing the amount equally between two funds. One fund tracked the S&P500, while the other tracked the NASDAQ100 index. Over the course of 18 years, these investments experienced an average annual growth of 12%. As a result, when Emma's child turned 18, the account had flourished into a remarkable sum of over £76,000. This significant amount was wisely allocated: a portion was utilised to cover the entire cost of university education, while the remaining funds served as a substantial deposit for purchasing a house. Emma's thoughtful actions have paved the way for her child's financial stability, ensuring a promising future.

2. **Junior SIPPs:** Consider the advantages of Junior SIPPs, which provide a long-term investment vehicle for children's retirement savings.

   Example: Recognising the importance of early retirement planning, David took a proactive step by establishing a Junior SIPP for his 10-year-old child. With a monthly contribution of £40, David aimed to lay a strong foundation for their future retirement fund. With the benefit of tax relief, the total contributions reached £50, which were then equally invested in funds tracking the S&P500 and the NASDAQ100. As the child reached the age of 18, the investments in the Junior SIPP had grown to just over £8,000. Although no further contributions were made after this milestone, the power of compounding continued to work its magic. By the time the child turned 60, their retirement fund had impressively multiplied, reaching a value of around £1.2 million. This remarkable outcome was solely achieved through David's consistent £40 monthly contributions to the Junior SIPP over the span of eight years. David's wise and disciplined approach to retirement planning has bestowed upon his child the gift of a comfortable retirement, highlighting the profound impact that consistent contributions, even in small amounts, can have over time when coupled with the benefits of tax relief and long-term investment growth.

Section 12.3: Transitioning Junior Accounts to Standard ISAs and SIPPs

As children transition to adulthood, it's crucial to guide them in managing their finances and transitioning their Junior accounts to standard ISAs and SIPPs. Here's how:

1. **Financial Education:** Educate your child about personal finance, investing, and the importance of long-term financial planning.

Example: Laura teaches her teenager about budgeting, investing in low-cost index funds, and the benefits of compounding growth.

2. **Account Transition:** Help your child transition their Junior ISA or Junior SIPP to a standard adult account when they reach the eligibility age.

Example: Mark provided guidance to his child in the crucial step of converting their Junior SIPP into a standard adult SIPP, enabling them to continue growing their retirement savings. Consequently, Mark ceased the monthly contributions of £80 into his child's SIPP. With an initial balance of £10,000, the child took the proactive decision to maintain a steady contribution of £80 per month during their time as a student and continued this practice throughout their career. The dedication to consistent savings paid off tremendously. Upon reaching the milestone of their 60th birthday, the child's SIPP account had remarkably grown to a substantial value exceeding £3 million! This impressive outcome underscores the profound impact of diligent contributions and long-term planning. Mark's guidance and the child's commitment to building their retirement fund have paved the way for a secure and financially abundant future.

Conclusion:

Building generational wealth involves thoughtful planning and strategic decision-making to pass on wealth effectively. By planning for beneficiaries, setting up accounts for children such as Junior ISAs and Junior SIPPs, and guiding the transition of these accounts to standard ISAs and SIPPs at adulthood, you can establish a strong financial foundation for future generations. Remember, the key is to instil financial education and empower your children to make informed financial decisions as they navigate their financial journeys.

CHAPTER XIII
SUMMARY OF RECOMMENDED ACCOUNTS

*A*s you embark on your journey towards financial well-being, it's crucial to understand the variety of accounts available to help you achieve your financial goals. In this chapter, we will provide a brief summary of the recommended accounts tailored to different financial objectives as mentioned throughout this book. We will highlight the benefits, eligibility criteria, and contribution strategies for each account type, empowering you to make informed decisions about your financial future.

Section 13.1: Emergency Fund Accounts

Building an emergency fund is crucial for financial security. Here are the recommended accounts for your emergency fund:

1. **High-Interest Savings Accounts:** These accounts offer competitive interest rates and

easy access to funds, making them ideal for short-term savings.

Benefits: Higher interest rates than traditional savings accounts, liquidity, and FSCS protection.

Eligibility: Generally open to UK residents aged 16 and above.

Contribution Strategy: Aim to save three to six months' worth of living expenses.

2. **Cash ISAs:** These tax-efficient savings accounts allow you to save a certain amount tax-free each year.

Benefits: Tax-free interest on savings and FSCS protection.

Eligibility: Open to UK residents aged 16 and above.

Contribution Strategy: Regularly contribute a portion of your income towards your emergency fund while taking advantage of the tax benefits.

Section 13.2: Retirement Accounts

Planning for retirement is crucial for long-term financial security. Here are the recommended retirement accounts:

1. **Workplace Pension Schemes:** These employer-sponsored pension schemes enable you to save for retirement with contributions from both you and your employer.

   Benefits: Tax relief on contributions, potential employer matching, and long-term growth.

   Eligibility: Offered by many employers in the UK; eligibility criteria vary.

   Contribution Strategy: Contribute at least enough to receive the full employer match.

2. **Personal Pensions (Stakeholder Pensions or Self-Invested Personal Pensions):** These individual pension accounts offer flexibility and tax advantages.

   Benefits: Tax relief on contributions, tax-deferred growth, and a wide range of investment options.

   Eligibility: Open to UK residents aged 18 and above.

   Contribution Strategy: Maximise your annual contributions to take full advantage of the tax benefits.

Section 13.3: Investment Accounts

Investing can help grow your wealth over the long term. Here are the recommended investment accounts:

1. **Stocks and Shares ISAs:** These tax-efficient investment accounts allow you to invest in a variety of assets, such as stocks, bonds, and funds.

    Benefits: Tax-free growth and tax-free withdrawals.

    Eligibility: Open to UK residents aged 18 and above.

    Contribution Strategy: Regularly contribute to take advantage of long-term investment growth.

2. **Lifetime ISAs:** These accounts offer tax-free growth and a government bonus for saving towards a first home or retirement.

    Benefits: Tax-free growth, government bonus, and flexibility for saving towards a first home or retirement.

    Eligibility: Open to UK residents aged 18 to 39.

    Contribution Strategy: Contribute regularly to maximise the government bonus and work towards your savings goals.

Section 13.4: *Junior Savings and Investment Accounts*

Planning for your child's future is an important aspect of building generational wealth. Here are the recommended junior accounts:

1. **Junior Cash ISAs:** These tax-efficient savings accounts allow parents or guardians to save on behalf of their child.

    Benefits: Tax-free interest on savings and FSCS protection.

    Eligibility: Available for children under the age of 18 and must be opened by a parent or legal guardian.

    Contribution Strategy: Regularly contribute to help your child build savings for their future.

2. **Junior Stocks and Shares ISAs:** These tax-efficient investment accounts allow parents or guardians to invest on behalf of their child.

    Benefits: Tax-free growth and tax-free withdrawals.

    Eligibility: Available for children under the age of 18 and must be opened by a parent or legal guardian.

    Contribution Strategy: Regularly contribute to harness the power of long-term investments for your child's future.

3. **Junior Self-Invested Personal Pensions (SIPPs):** These individual pension accounts can help secure your child's financial future.

   Benefits: Tax relief on contributions, tax-deferred growth, and a wide range of investment options.

   Eligibility: Available for children under the age of 18 and must be opened by a parent or legal guardian.

   Contribution Strategy: Contribute regularly to maximise the long-term growth potential of the pension account.

Conclusion:

Understanding the various accounts available for different financial goals is crucial for effective financial planning. By considering the recommended accounts outlined in this chapter, such as emergency fund accounts, retirement accounts, and investment accounts, you can align your savings and investment strategies with your objectives. Remember to review the eligibility criteria, contribution strategies, and benefits of each account type to make informed decisions that align with your financial goals.

CHAPTER XIV
CALCULATING YOUR SAVINGS TARGETS

*C*alculating your savings targets is a crucial part of effective financial planning. In this chapter, we will guide you through the process of determining your savings targets for various financial goals, including retirement planning, saving for a home deposit, and setting up junior accounts. By following the step-by-step instructions and considering relevant factors, you can calculate the monthly savings amounts needed to achieve your specific targets.

Section 14.1: Retirement Savings Targets

When calculating your retirement savings target, consider the following factors:

- Determine your desired retirement age.

- Estimate your expected annual retirement expenses, considering factors like lifestyle and healthcare costs.

- Determine the duration of your retirement based on your life expectancy.

- Consider the potential growth of your investments over time, keeping in mind historical average returns.

- Adjust your retirement savings target to account for the impact of inflation on future expenses.

Example: Suppose you have set a retirement age of 65, and currently, you're 25 years old, with estimated annual retirement expenses of £30,000. To determine the monthly savings amount required to reach your retirement goal, you can utilise online retirement calculators or financial planning tools.

The first step involves calculating the target value of your retirement fund by the time you retire to generate the desired income. Assuming an average annual investment return of 6%, we divide £30,000 by 6% to arrive at a figure of £500,000.

Next, utilising the "monthly payment calculator" on thecalculatorsire.com, input the savings goal of £500,000, annual returns of 6%, and a timeframe of 40 years. This yields a required monthly deposit of £251.07.

To factor in tax relief, deduct 20% from this figure, resulting in an actual monthly contribution required from you of £200.86.

To account for inflation, it's recommended to increase your contributions by 2% annually. This adjustment ensures that when you reach retirement, your pension account will generate sufficient income to offset any effects of inflation.

By following these steps and consistently contributing towards your retirement fund, you can work towards achieving your financial goals and securing a comfortable retirement.

Section 14.2: Home Deposit Savings Targets

When saving for a home deposit, consider the following aspects:

- Determine the price range of the property you want to purchase.

- Calculate the loan-to-value ratio (LTV) required by lenders, typically ranging from 5% to 20%.

- Set a target timeframe for saving the deposit based on your property purchase timeline.

- Divide the required deposit amount by the number of months in your timeframe to determine the monthly savings goal.

- Account for any government bonuses you may be getting in your account

Example: Suppose your goal is to save a £25,000 deposit for a property priced at £250,000 within a timeframe of 5 years. To accomplish this, you would need to save £417 per month. By utilising a Lifetime ISA, you can take advantage of a 25% government bonus on your savings. As a result, the actual monthly contribution into your Lifetime ISA would be £333.60 to reach the desired amount for your deposit.

By leveraging the benefits of a Lifetime ISA and diligently saving the adjusted monthly contribution, you can steadily work towards achieving your goal of securing the deposit for your dream property.

Section 14.3: Junior Account Savings Targets

When setting up junior accounts, such as Junior ISAs or Junior SIPPs, consider the following:

- Determine your long-term savings goals for your child, such as education expenses or a deposit for their first home.

- Determine the number of years until the funds will be required.

- Consider the potential growth of investments within the junior account over the investment timeframe.

Example: Suppose your goal is to save £30,000 for your child's university education in a span of 18 years. To determine the required monthly savings amount, you can invest in a Junior ISA with an assumed average growth rate of 5%.

By utilising the "monthly payment calculator" on thecalculatorsite.com, you can calculate that the necessary monthly deposit to reach your target is £85.91. This is the amount you will need to contribute to the Junior ISA on a monthly basis to achieve your goal.

By consistently making the calculated monthly deposits into the Junior ISA, you can work towards accumulating the desired funds for your child's future university education. This proactive approach to saving will provide them with financial support and opportunities for a bright academic journey.

Conclusion:

Calculating your savings targets is an essential part of financial planning. By considering factors like retirement age, expenses, investment growth, and property purchase goals, you can determine the monthly savings amounts required to achieve your desired outcomes. Whether it's planning for retirement, saving for a home deposit, or setting up junior accounts, the step-by-step instructions and utilisation of online tools will help you stay on track and make informed decisions about your savings strategy.

CHAPTER XV
CELEBRATING MILESTONES &
REWARDS

*I*n the journey towards financial success, it's essential to not only focus on the end goal but also acknowledge and celebrate the milestones along the way. In this chapter, we'll delve into the significance of recognising and celebrating financial milestones and how small rewards can help motivate and propel you towards achieving your goals. By embracing the concept of celebrating milestones, you can enhance your financial journey and foster a positive mindset towards long-term financial success.

Section 15.1: Importance of Recognising Financial Milestones

- Acknowledge the progress made in your financial journey, such as paying off debts, reaching savings targets, or achieving investment milestones.

- Celebrate milestones as a way to boost morale, maintain motivation, and sustain momentum in your financial endeavours.

- Reflect on the positive changes and improvements you have made in your financial habits and decisions.

Section 15.2: Small Rewards for Achieving Goals

- Consider incorporating small rewards or treats to mark the achievement of specific financial goals.

- Set milestone-based rewards that align with your personal preferences and interests.

- Ensure the rewards are within your budget and do not hinder your progress towards broader financial goals.

Example: If you successfully pay off a significant portion of your debt, reward yourself with a weekend getaway or a nice dinner at your favourite restaurant. These small treats can serve as reminders of your accomplishments and provide a well-deserved break from the rigors of financial discipline.

Section 15.3: Psychological Benefits of Rewards

- Rewards reinforce positive financial behaviours and create a sense of satisfaction and accomplishment.

- They help combat burnout or discouragement during challenging times, providing an incentive to keep going.

- Celebrating milestones can create a positive association with financial progress and foster a healthier relationship with money.

Example: Suppose you've achieved a savings target for a specific purpose, such as a dream vacation. Treating yourself to a memorable experience not only celebrates your financial success but also encourages you to continue making smart financial decisions in the future.

Conclusion:

Celebrating milestones and rewarding yourself along your financial journey is an integral part of maintaining motivation and sustaining progress. By recognising and celebrating financial achievements, you create a positive mindset that supports long-term financial success. Small rewards and treats act as reminders of your dedication and accomplishments, providing both psychological and emotional benefits. So, as you make progress towards your financial goals, remember to take the time to celebrate milestones and reward yourself for your hard work and dedication.

CONCLUSION

Throughout this book, we've explored a wide range of financial topics, strategies, and tools aimed at helping you achieve financial freedom and build a secure future. As we wrap up our journey together, let's take a moment to recap the key points and concepts covered and reinforce the importance of taking action to implement these strategies in your own life.

We started by emphasising the significance of setting clear financial goals and creating a solid foundation for your financial journey. From managing debt and maximising savings to exploring various investment options, we've provided practical insights and actionable steps to guide you along the way.

It's essential to remember that financial success is not an overnight endeavour, but rather a continuous journey that requires commitment and discipline. By making sound financial decisions, prioritising savings, and investing wisely, you can pave the way for a brighter financial future.

Now is the time to put what you've learned into action. Take the knowledge and strategies shared in this book and apply them to your own unique circumstances. Tailor these concepts to fit your goals, lifestyle, and aspirations. Whether you're just starting out or well on your way, every step you take towards financial empowerment is a step closer to achieving your dreams.

As you embark on this journey, remember that it's normal to encounter challenges and setbacks along the way. Financial success is not without its hurdles, but with resilience, determination, and the knowledge you've gained, you have the power to overcome them.

I am optimistic about your future. I believe that by implementing the strategies and principles discussed in this book, you have the ability to transform your financial well-being and build generational wealth. Stay focused, stay motivated, and never lose sight of the goals you've set for yourself.

Thank you for joining me on this exploration of personal finance. Remember, financial freedom is within your reach. The choices you make today will shape the trajectory of your financial future. Take control, make informed decisions, and embrace the journey towards financial independence.

Wishing you success, abundance, and a lifetime of financial freedom.

Hassan Afifi

ABOUT THE AUTHOR

Hassan Afifi is a UK-based investment professional. He started investing and trading in financial markets in the early 1990s while at university. He holds a BA in economics.

Hassan has worked in institutional equity sales, advising some of the world's largest fund managers on their investments across different geographies and sectors.

He has also worked in corporate finance, helping entrepreneurs start or grow their businesses, raise funds for their projects, and guide management teams through their financial planning processes.

Hassan returned to the investment world full-time in 2020 focusing on wealth management to try and help as many people as he can to achieve their financial freedom.

Printed in Great Britain
by Amazon